HOW TO
GET OVER A GUY
IN 10 DAYS

ISBN: 1-4196-5845-X

Acknowledgments

Jeannie and Michele would like to thank:

Our families for all their support and our
friends for all their inspiration.

Special thanks to:

Tyla Berchtold, Scott Leonard, Dorian Garcia
and Brian Alexander.

Finally, this book would not be possible without:

Adam, Bryan, David, Eric, Jason, John, Jonathan,
Marc, Mike, Rob, Stephen, Steve
and a few we can't remember.

HOW TO
GET OVER
A GUY
IN
10 DAYS

written by

Michele Alexander & Jeannie Long

DAY
1

Break up with him.

(He'll never do it - even if he's planning a
wedding with someone else)

No matter what you do...
don't cry in front of him.

Call every friend you've ever had. CRY.

Take back all the big ticket
items you bought him.

Leave the hottest picture of you
on his refrigerator.

(or somewhere he'll find it later)

Rip up all his old letters and
burn them.

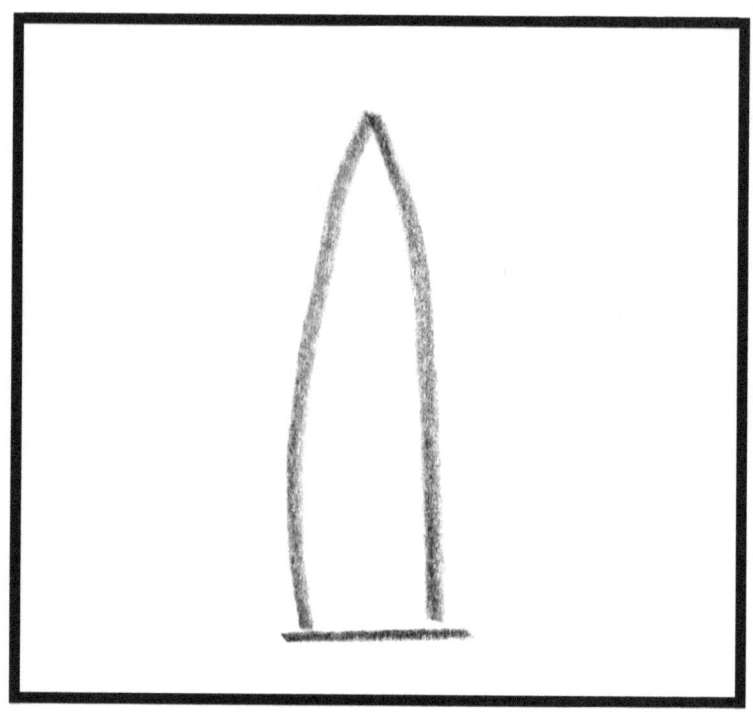

Buy a vibrator.

DAY
2

Stop taking the pill.

Get mad at your friends for not telling you sonner that he was a LOSER!

Start a diet.

Get your teeth whitened.

Color your hair. Go blonde!

Workout.

Practice your "get lost" speech for when he calls to get you back.

Go to a party.

Flirt with every guy there.

Cry when you see a couple
holding hands.

Drunk dial him.

Cry.

DAY
3

Only refer to him as
"The Asshole."

Have a post break-up wake.

(Have your friends bring beer)

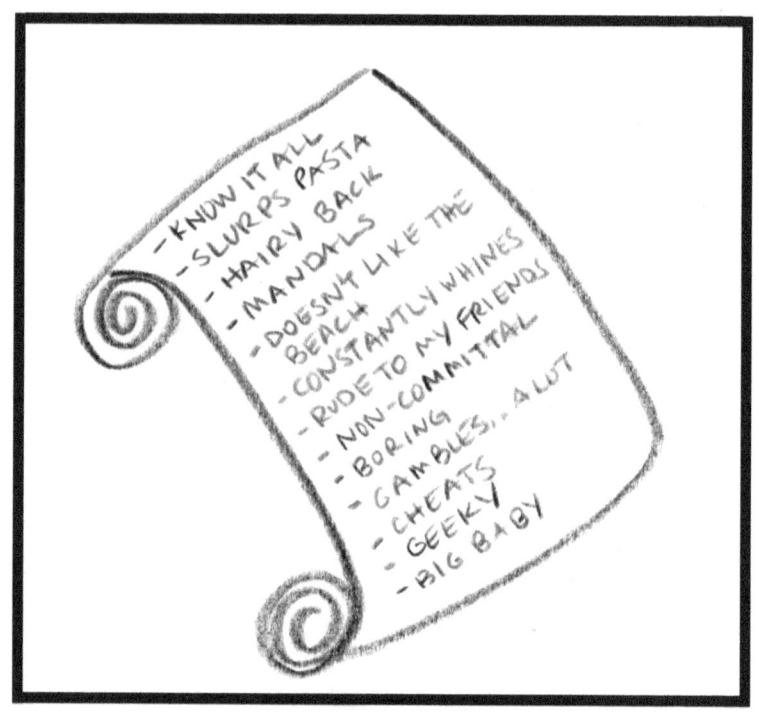

Make a list of all his annoying qualities. You don't want to date this guy again.

Throw away everything that
reminds you of him.

Give all stuffed animals he gave
you to your dog.

Bury all pictures of him in a
box.

Have your best friend tell you
what she *really* thinks.

Vow to never call him again.

Call him.

Cry.

DAY
4

Stare at yourself in the mirror and tell yourself that you're pretty.

Give his clothes to a homeless
person near his office.

Register at Target.
Leave groom blank.

Buy a voodoo doll.

Use it.

Call his friend who always
liked you.

Tell him how great you're doing.

Write him a letter telling him
everything.

Don't send it.

Tell your friends you can't go
out because you're journaling.

Call them back and ask them if they
want to hear what you wrote.

DAY
5

Resist ALL temptations...

NO drive bys.

NO listening to his messages.

NO reading his emails.

NO driving his convertible
into a ditch.

Instead, take the high road...

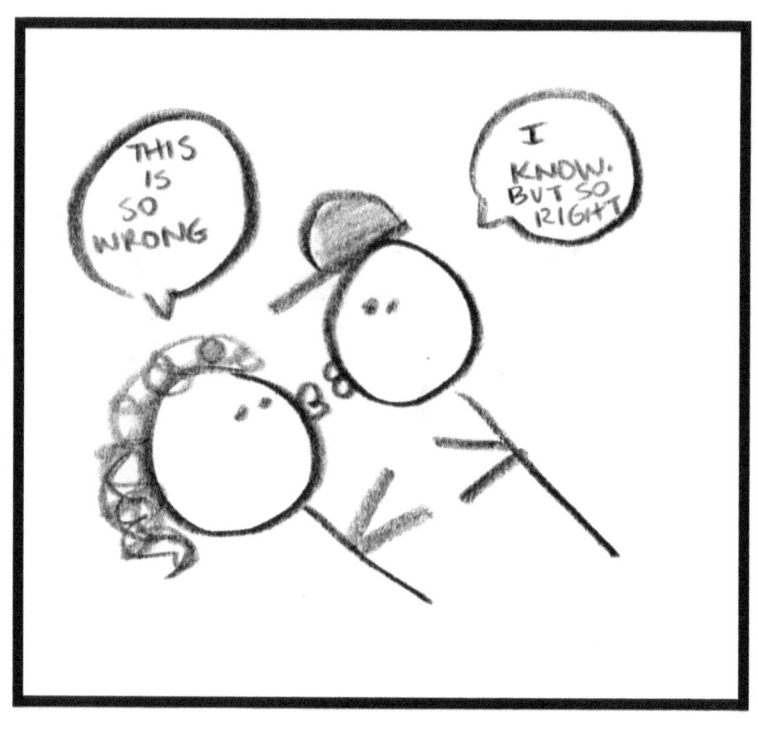

Have revenge sex with
his best friend.

DAY
6

Toss out your fat clothes.

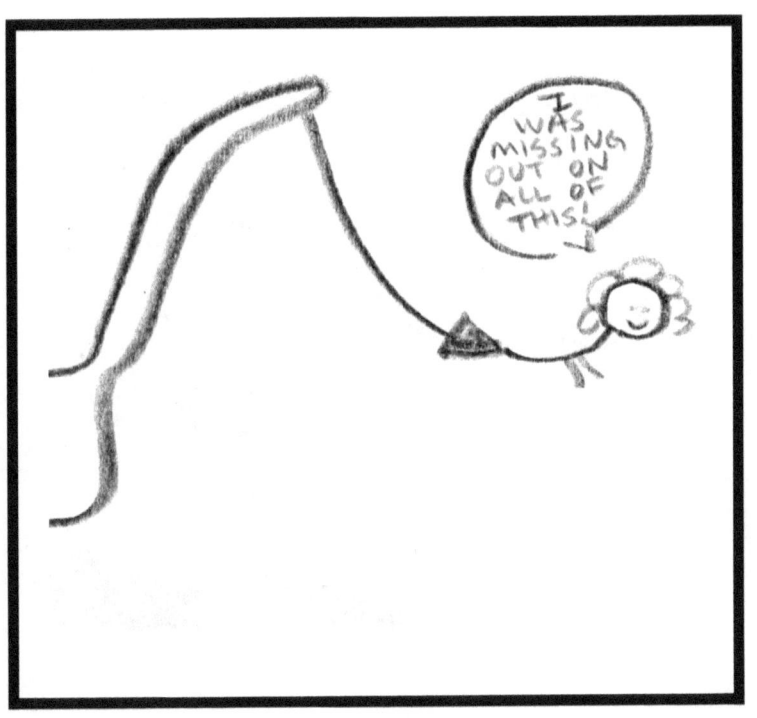

Start doing all the things he
wanted you to do.

(cook, watch porn, go to a baseball game,
consider a three way)

Remember all the bad things.

(He's cheap, the weird face he made when you had sex, the time he farted and said it was his shoe, his halitosis)

Write his mom a letter and tell her you're sorry that he's such a jerk.

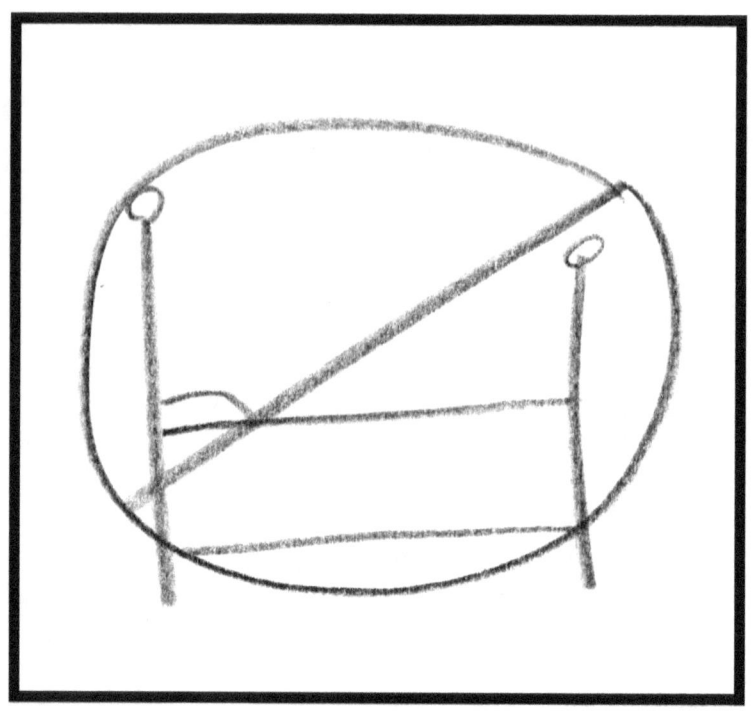

Stay away from places you used to hang out.

Claim all the good places and
leave him with the bad.

Rent "Unfaithful."

Get drunk with your friends.

Plan a huge revenge plot where
you pull out all the hair on his
arms one by one with tweezers.

DAY
7

Cancel plan.
You don't care anymore.

Loop "You Oughta Know" on your iPod.

Get hypnotized.

Block him from your buddy list.

Be inspired by J.Lo. She did it.

If he calls, pick up...then hang
up when he says, "Hello."

Tell someone who's never been in a relationship that it's better to have loved and lost, than to have never loved at all.

DAY
8

Stare at yourself in the mirror
and tell yourself you're pretty.

Start believing it.

Become spiritual.

Take up Kabbalah.

Volunteer.

Get a new piercing.

Learn a new language.

Start a philanthropy.

Tell your friends not to mention him again.

And, if you talk about him, make them charge you a dollar.

Have a party. Don't invite him.

Tell everyone that you just couldn't date someone who was "afraid of love."

DAY
9

Stop talking about him. When
anyone mentions his name,
start humming.

Embody a new theme song.

Flirt with someone online.

Walk by a construction site.

Go to a gay bar with your most
fabulous gay.

Let him compliment you
until you can't stand it anymore.

Erase all saved messages
from him.

Get in touch with back-ups.

DAY
10

Go on a self-healing retreat.

Become one with the earth.

Move to a new neighborhood.

Go on a date with a really nice
guy. Let him open the door for
you and say you're funny.

Don't tell him you're fresh
off a break-up.

(You are over him anyway)

When he asks to see you again,
say, "YES!"

Erase "The Asshole's" number.

Believe that he was just a
stepping stone and the
universe was just preparing you
for something better.

Books also written by this author:

How to Lose a Guy in 10 Days
How to Tell He's Not the One in 10 Days
How to Get a Guy in 10 Days

Available on Amazon.com and other major booksellers.

For more information, please contact
HowToIn10Days@gmail.com.

www.ingramcontent.com/pod-product-compliance
Lightning Source LLC
Chambersburg PA
CBHW030401290526
45785CB00004B/1850